The Clattering
Voices from Old Forfarshire, Scotland

The Clattering
Voices from Old Forfarshire, Scotland

Poems by Sherri Bedingfield

GRAYSON BOOKS
WEST HARTFORD, CT
www.GraysonBooks.com

Bedingfield, Sherri, author.
    [Poems. Selections]
    The clattering : voices from Old Forfarshire,
  Scotland : poems / by Sherri Bedingfield.
    pages cm
    ISBN 978-0-9962809-4-5

    1. Witchcraft--Scotland--Poetry.   I. Title.

  PS3602.E343A6 2016   811'.6
                                QBI16-600052

Book & Cover Design by Cindy Mercier
Cover Artwork by Sherri Bedingfield
Author Photo by Christine Beck

GraysonBooks.com

In Appreciation

Many thanks and much gratitude to my friends and colleagues who have constantly supported me in my development as a poet. In addition I want to thank the folks at Grayson Books for their patience, skill and encouragement in bringing this book to life. Thanks also to my dear poetry group, the Pips, for their critique and support over the years: Christine Beck, Ginny Connors, Tere Foley, Nancy Kerrigan, Pat Hale, Julia Paul, and Elaine Zimmerman. I want to thank Marilyn Johnston and Rhett Watts for their sensitive insights and encouragement. Thanks to Suzy Lamson, Shelly Weinberg, and Tom Nicotera for an insightful evening of role play based on these poems. And thanks to Christine Beck for her photograph of the author.

Isobel

Isobel Shyrie walked through angled morning light,
under oak, white willow and apple trees, stepped
over slabs of stone on the path toward Loch Forfar.
Forest still cool, shadowed from night's air, birds chanting,
a cacophony. Filled her pockets with glistening berries—
and for that hour, forgot that she was a poor woman, almost old.

Hungry children waited in kitchens, sat on oak benches
and in willow chairs, faced their mother's or grandmother's backs,
saw stoves burn with small fires and slabs of cut bacon
to be browned up, served with richly seasoned sliced potatoes.

Her August gardens, fat and full—garlic, dandelion,
yellow yarrow, nasturtium, nettle, and sage—waved under bees—
grown for the families, the good neighbors, the people of Forfar,
their food, their medicine for the coming dark winter.
Isobel, not yet a crone, saw no sign of the change
that would come, the change that would pursue her.

Contents

Introduction
Forfarshire, Scotland 1663

Forfar Castle, one of King Malcolm's castles, had defended Scotland
from Danish invaders. The region surrounding the castle was known as
Forfarshire. By the time Isobel Shyrie and Helen Guthrie were
living, it had long been demolished and lay in chunks scattered across
the county. Isobel, Helen and a number of their peers were eventually
judged and condemned in Forfarshire Township.

The poems in this collection are about these women and others in
Forfarshire, or Forfar, as the town is called today. During those difficult
years of religious wars, the Reformation, and Black Plague, the
population was fearful. It wasn't difficult for the powerful to manipulate
others in order to gain land or money, or control the villagers. The time
was three years before the famous fires that burned London.

The poems collected here are about real people. They are a blend of
historical fact and imagined details.

Hope

Isobel and Ian, Early On

Across the table his shoulders
silhouetted
by the fading sun.
Across the table he held his
cup of beer
in a square hand she would
remember all her years.

Her fingers rested on purple grapes,
not eating only waiting
for her next cue
her skin warm as summer,
his eyes adoring—
she breathed him in.

Like a course of fire
the two of them would
burn and turn
and spin through their first months.

In a Stone Cottage on an Unnamed Road

Bent from green willow, a cradle
for his baby, little one with tangled curls.
The father, just a boy himself, shaped it.

A straw-grass mattress held the mother,
her new born daughter at her side-
tiny thing, rose face, balled fists.

Pot of stew at low fire, her sister's gift.
Breasts, milk-heavy. The feel of breath—
this tiny thing. Rosy face, round head.

Chest of hope, hope chest.
Quiet as grass at early morning-
drowsy mother, sleeping baby,

black curls on muslin cheesecloth.
Newborn in green willow cradle.
Wealth of wood for winter at the doorway.

Thank God for it. Smell of willow,
potatoes with lamb and garlic. Margaret newborn
hope—the mother's life unfolding before her.

Isobel, Entranced

Your eyes, clear
and new, are you
seeing me?
my gentle glance,

all that we are
is one long moment
or moment
after moment
how do you see it?

Baby my baby
remember
your turn in my
belly? These
heavy breasts
pull down to you.

Your black curls
rosy skin,
a turn of light
my rush
to your cry.

Our closeness,
a threshold
a thin place
divinity.

What more
could I want?

The Disappearance

Crossing the muggy marsh,
Ian's horse broke into gallop,
wild rider, he leaned over
the gray's flying mane.

Ian and the horse galloped north,
kicked up red stones
from peat fields
charged the rolling hills
like they were flat and nothing,
like he was the only rider
in the world that last day.

On horseback Ian felt his power,
curly hair flying, he and the horse
silhouetted in horizon's glow
from an orange sun.

His brother promised something.
Was this reconciliation?
After years, had Alec at last put his hate aside?

Isobel comfortable,
not knowing how soon the end
would come for him, rocked
their daughter in a willow cradle
beside the hearth.

She smiled to herself, waited
for her husband's return,
watched the sinking sun,
and her baby sleeping.

The Villagers' Voices 1

There was always trouble
between the brothers, though Ian
had tried and tried. He wondered
could things change?

Alec's family prepared a feast.
For days they planned, did you hear this?
Fresh fruits in glass bowls,
red and white meats.

Dried flowers, dark wines, many sweets.
At a stone hearth, the fire crackled
comfort. Ian sipped wine,
his niece played at his feet.

The poison wine betrayed him.
Murdered, Ian is no more.
Did you hear that he is gone?

Forever disappeared. Buried deep
in a bog of peat.
For weeks, only his horse knew it.

Thorns

She Could Have Been Pretty

As a girl she was a storm in her mother's house.
Angry at everything, even the day itself
or the sky.

She always thought pucas were crawling on her
and it was her sister's fault. She could have been
pretty if she held her face a different way. Awake

late through the night, she had her dark thoughts.
Stared at her sister sleeping. She never forgot anything
she ever thought about.

At her best, she sang with her head up and her eyes
focused to a distance. Helen was not gentle, no,
she didn't smile anything like a real smile.

Her mother found her sister dead, eyes open,
on the back porch in her wicker chair. Helen wearing
her Sunday dress, knife in her pocket.
Singing to the kitchen. No one ever accused her.

Like the Other Stones

People closed their windows
        closed their doors under a mercurial red moon.

Not Helen. Her door wide open,
        like her eyes, through the whole night.

To herself she smiled, darkly.
        Finally her sister was a stone like all the other
        stones.

The murder happened under blue
        morning skies.

Helen at Twenty

Not available. Not avoidable.
Only a rare profile, a curve of her neck
        as auburn hair curled around it,
        a glance of glamour.

Commonly, a distance held
her gaze, as if she saw someone,
something no one else could see.
        A fright she was
        and few caught her eyes or wanted to.

Isobel, fearless, saw
Helen's strength beyond
        her darkness—like thorns
        protecting kits in a thicket.

A man was there once
and Helen softened. He almost claimed
        her with his patience. Still she kept
        her guard, like the thorns, sharp,
        never different, distant, she finally made
        him leave.

Baillie George, Early Morning

Hunger was a separate entity inside him and it didn't always want food. This morning he was hungry and cold. He pulled a heavy shirt around his shoulders. Wifey had closed up the worn elbows. Good, at least she would fix his things. In the kitchen he stood before the stove fire, took an apple from the oak table, was aware he munched it like a horse would do. He moved to the east window facing the street. Saw her first thing: Isobel, slipping up the hill again as if she were a weightless cloud, as if she were a sassy breeze with her brown basket of nettles and comfrey and whatever else she stuffed into it—surely beetles were in the dirty roots and stems. Women liked her though. Her tinctures, the herbs and leaves stopped children's fevers, comfrey soothed their bellies when they ate their Ma's burnt cooking. Even Wifey liked her. At the sight of Isobel his skin still prickled. She was the first woman he'd ever wanted. All those years ago she turned a cold shoulder to him, a November night it was. He had just wanted to touch her yellow hair. He remembered how his face flushed, and it burned now. She'd become a widow, no family left he knew of. Wait, no, she had a daughter, a stretch of land. Isobel went to the women when they bled, when they had their babies. Did she have the inky blue evil eye? He thinks the Father thinks it. Seeing her squint is a sure sign. In a dream last week she placed her arms on his shoulders until he felt his power drain away— Aye, slipped through the bottoms of his feet. Slipped out the ends of his fingers. He saw her thin image at the foot of his bed in the wee hours.

Planning the Plantings

Isobel met Helen and Janet for years behind the church,
the kirk, shaded with old oaks, under round faced
and sickle moons—

vast orb of dreams; days were counted between
the full and the dark, the waxing gibbous: a meditation
for seeds of plenty. Flat moon, it did what it did.

Old January moon, Wolf Moon, waited. Blocked
by clouds, dubious weather, no matter. Direction came
from its slant of light, its shade of shadow.

Daughters from town and her own daughter, Margaret
joined them for April's Pink Moon with clear nights.
Three days it glowed, showed three days red, three days
it went to dark—

and the ground softened. The signs, markers in time.
Force of dawn, dawn of force—pale orb, plate of plenty.
Caped in gray fog, morning opened, a silver edge.

Moon set west with darkness. Moon first, ocean followed.
Water on sand and stone—lunar ebbs and starts.
Prayers for plenty.

Isobel, Helen and Janet, the oldest three, confident.
Margaret danced the side path behind the kirk,
waved her long blue skirt.

At a Window

Morning silence
in the shiver of March.
A gray-yellow finch

and song sparrows
arrive. They dive
before a clattering

of sooty jackdaws
re-arrange themselves
in a black oak, shifting

their sharp gray eyes
for anything. Slips
of cheese and bread crusts

draw them down
to find the thistle seed
Isobel bundled in cheesecloth.

Here is winter's turn
from weariness—
the birds come.

Ice at the north side
of barns and cottages
breaks apart—

the edges of puddles
and lochs soften.
Asparagus and kale

push through earth's
thawing crusts. The days
add their minutes again.

April Planting

Margaret hummed,
Isobel sang.
They cleaned surfaces
with hot water
from the cauldron over fire
after eating lamb stew.
Cleaned plates and cups
in a sun-bleached kitchen
turned blue by evening.

Last season's seeds waited
over the cold months
for this night
to be planted
under April's pink moon.

Ash

His Long Shadow

George Wood, Tax Collector

He walked with heavy feet, shoulders down.
A tall man, focused, no meandering.
Cold eyes, cold for those he didn't like. Kicked up stones
in front of their doors. He had his reasons.

Pressed his face up to their windows, eyes cold,
claimed they had his money, didn't pay their due.
His heavy walk warned them—
women kept their distance.

George dragged his feet,
flattened seedlings, nasturtium and nettle,
kicked up onions, crushed potatoes.
His long shadow—women watched for it.

Beware, keep back.
Relentless, his heavy feet.
When stones moved,
the women had their signs, their signals.

George at Night's Middle

George woke at night's middle
almost every night, thinking
of who lived where, who owned what.
Forfarshire's wood paths,
its roads and streets; in his mind's eye
the land spread wide, a gold-green
haze, a blanket, a breeze,
a maze of grains waving.

Fields filled his dreams, land
for a kingdom from heaven—
treasure to the kirkyard. The priest
should get his parcel. George dreamed
he was the town hero.

They owed him, those women,
Isobel, her friends, and Helen the strange.
The church needed its land—those women
expect him to let them off every quarter.
Years have passed between payments.
As tax agent, their land is his.

In his next dream George received
a gift before the town—a blue cape
placed around his shoulders.
He felt his chest swell.
The dream showed he was not a dark man,
not greedy as some said.

The last dream offered a treasure
hidden in the field. A man with a tall collar
found it. In the distance George could see
him smiling as he covered it over.
The dream was clear—the Father's gratitude
would bring George many blessings.

A Spell in Forfarshire

Against Baillie George Wood, tax collector who harassed poor women

We say   you are not forgiven
we turn three times   call up the darkness—
shadows creep and crawl to you by sunrise
            spread like webbing
about your bed   your head   around your house
knock knock   turn three times   together   we say.

Shadows cover over your land   blanket your garden
eat your seeds   and return nothing. And there is more.
The floors in your house soften   they twist
            tomorrow the house leans
            the seventh day it starts to sink.
Rain will knock   rap-tapping every window.
Wind will snare your shutters.

Who will care?
Your head aches and you don't understand.
Fear swells   narrows your throat.
            Not to be forgiven   you won't.
            No one cares.

Food in your belly sours   a scent collects around you
turns foul.
The skin of your face reddens with fevers
            cools chalk white, withers.
            Withers again.

Ash on you. Ash in the air makes fibers   tiny sticks
in your lungs stiffen.   Your throat swells
knock knock   cough and rattle
            turn three times.
            Your family   your lovers
betray you   lift their shoulders   turn away.
You are not forgiven   *spin three times*

35

The coins you took from poor women
        all the money   again and again
your face loomed at our windows   your lips open.
Years of taxes   the money burns   burns each place you hide it—
your fingers singe   they shrivel   we turn and spin
        to you the shadows crawl   to you like webbing
        knock knock, knock.

George Is Found

The first window had lifted from its frame,
　　　　slightly twisted.

Afternoon sunlight spilled over
　　warped floorboards in a cold hallway.
　　Kitchen chairs upside down
　　around the wall in what had been
　　a gathering room—

its windows fogged from a cold
　　that casts winter inside the house.
　　Floors a man could barely walk
　　without being sucked to sinking.

The house was stormed even though
　　no storms had come.
　　The back, the kitchen greeted
　　Father Peter with fetid smells.

Pots and spoons across the floor,
　　then the Priest saw him there, George
　　white and withered against the door—
　　the body of George,
　　never to be anyone, anymore.

The Villagers' Voices 2

A gathering of hares almost never happens
in the wild woods or any other place.
And if it has, no one ever claimed to see them.
At least no person—maybe the jackdaws of the field
or a cat in the low grass might tell of such a thing,
if they could speak. You've never seen a gathering
of hares, have you?

Still the stories tell of hares gathered in silent circles
staring at each other across the air between them.
Staring and staring. There must have been something
to it. A wise old man had a tale of them. He walked
the town twice each day to see if there was cause
for suspicion. Once, walking past the church he saw
two men and several women gathered there. An air
of the unusual between them.

He could see one of the women clearly—
Wifey, the tax collector's wife with her hair down
and wearing a blue cape. Standing, they were,
maybe about to enter the back door for a Kirk session.
A neighbor took his eyes briefly, a small moment—
when he glanced back to the entryway
the people were gone. Long-legged hares
leaped and scampered in zig-zags toward the woods.

Such a scene—in a blink, a mere wink,
the wild rabbits disappeared.
He had a strange feeling when he saw the blue cape
caught in a thicket. The long-legged hares,
could they have been shape-shifters?
The wise old man pondered it, his lips pursed.

Moon Watch

They sit and wait for it—
   the orange hunter's moon
   edged by purple-fingered
clouds.
   It floats afire
   over sleeping birds
huddled like winter's come

a line of them, silhouettes
   on a middle branch
   of the black oak.

      ***

January moon predicts
   an unclear future—
     a map to lure them
   a marker, a guide
     in time, out of time,
out of reason.

A sliver of light
     barely there
   or full circle moon,
like a white plate
   milk faced
   over jackdaws at dawn
     grazing the fields.

Isobel's Luminous Dream

In the dream some were uneasy
but others knew the sounds.
They heard the wailing for themselves,
were wise like the old ones.
The townspeople gathered
at the gloaming on their green
and made a fire to spring.

Isobel could hear the trees calling.
The oaks first as their roots thickened.
Spring's soil had softened.
Even the Father heard them—
he nodded to her grandmother
whose eyes were glowing.

In the body of the old trees
certain souls found their places.
In her dream Isobel and Reverend
saw spirits taken up by the oaks
like water pulled from earth.

Those who died beside the road,
in their fields, or died in child-birth
animated the oaks.
New roots pushed down and leaf buds
fattened. Her mother, long passed

stood at the grove's edge in a blue dress
with her blond hair braided
holding Margaret's hand.
Ground winds whipped cold air
over summer's cornlands. In the dream
she knew that nurture
would declare the summer's harvest.

Isobel's Husband Returns

She never thought it would come
to this—her bringing him back
or that he could come back at all.

Her eyes were wide as if she'd
never slept—no shaft of light
let her see him, yet he had come.

And she did see him. Had she
conjured him up in her dream?
The air that was him became

dense, thickened around her.
Like a fog he was gathered—
collected over her, in front

of her, she could breathe him
in. Her dead husband had become
a mist over her bed.

In a glance this airy weight
slipped away from her to hover
at the doorway, to venture outside.

The moon must have pulled him away.

Isobel to Margaret

My girl, beloved,
what we had with your Da'
until the poison took him.
He made your first bed
from softened willow.

His tangled curls twist
in grace about your face,
his rosy cheeks shine
above your smile.

We have what we have—
enough memories
under this blank sky
before the jackdaw walks
its fields.

Last night your father stood,
he did,
at the foot of my bed—
shoulders square, tall again,

He didn't speak. I thought
he would, thought he'd dare
slip in with me, our bed.
It could have been yesterday.

He looked like he did
when he was with us.
I wanted
to call you, my girl,
till the dream faded him thin.

Woe

A Fire Goes Out

In the 1600's in Scotland, it was essential to keep the family fire going.

Distracted girl, the fire low or dead,
Ma would choke her for it. Cold air
and the stench of peat ashes offered
a surprising smell of decay.

The smell woke her in early afternoon.
Distracted girl, her mother's voice.
She'd listened to the wind, avoided chores.
An unexpected sleep took her,

took the morning. Cold and wind
lulled her, later it woke her. The raucous
whisper and spit of fire's tongues
seeking air gone silent.

Her fault, her fault it was. Where was mother?
The fire's dead or low and Ma could choke her.
Never let a fire die, distracted girl—
never had till then. Wind lulled her. The smell
woke her in early afternoon. Her skin cold.

Fire's hissing whisper, its spitting tongues gone.
She could gather leaves and prickly sticks
dry as dust from under the lean-to, mound ashes and peat
to hearth's center, make a flame. Hot coals buried

under ash, they must be there, she'd seen it done.
Use her flimsy slip, cloth so soft, a tear of linen,
cover it with ash. Margaret would make her flame
or Ma would choke her for it.

The Fever in Edinburgh

Postings on the alehouses
and front doors of churches—
no congregating
only for praying.
Contagions creep over the streets.
They say infection floats
as miasmic clouds.
Plague has struck the city.

Dear Lord
I am not always good
with my prayers to you.
Forgive me. Please
keep the pestilence
from our town
form our home
from my beloved daughter.

They are burying the bodies
in one huge pit
where they will burn.
Contagion creeps.
Lord
I pray for all souls.

Father Peter Dreamed

a fire with blue-orange tongues, a pale woman,
   a gray skirt, like burned ash, a brown belt
   at her waist; a dark worm.

A torn fence in both her hands under blood moon
   beasts flew over her head, over the Village—

Tipped graves, browned wheat, killed
   cows, chicks at her feet. He had seen them
   all before. Woe, woe, the face was Isobel's.

A Priest Condemns

The church a somber building
numinous as afternoon sun
brightened the small nave,
spilling white light
down narrow aisles
from small high windows.

After the heavy double doors
where the parish entered
candles were stationed on wooden
mounts behind shallow pews
and straight-backed chairs.

Reverend's words were clear—
they were the King James' words
She would rise in the thin air
alongside the dark ones.
Aye, like burned ash on a cold hearth
they lifted. Every day her hair twisted
thick and thicker like dense
and wild ivy—
her voice would call up the beasts.

Open your eye in night's middle,
her image sits at the side of your bed.
Find a woman that opens her door
with a pot on her fire—she will be
the devil's wife, strange and waiting
to brown your crops, sicken your children,
sink your ships. A witch tried to sink mine!

Father Peter sat in his high-backed chair
and reflected in the dim light of the vestry.
Tomorrow the people would arrive early
for prayer, for praise, for listening.

The Villagers' Voices 3

Did you hear? Did you hear him?
Father Peter, now
he is the King's voice.

The King's words spill from
the Father's mouth. What woman
in all of Forfar would not have
a pot on her fire? Which one?

Her family must eat and bathe.
King's words say any woman
with a pot on her fire is evil
so all are. The rich be the only

innocent, they touch no pot, fondle
no fire. King's words say the women
rise and fly, the devil's wives they are.

King says the women follow him
with dark words, with curses. They look like
gray ash from a cold hearth on the other side
of their beauty.

Women sink the king's ships, the last
almost went under twice. Children
are stricken, they sicken—
Did you hear?

Helen Meets a Town Constable Outside the Toll House

I know things, Helen said.
He stood back under shadow, kept clear of her.
    If I tell, will you protect me?

I heard about your cow she said in a whisper to pull him closer,
    and your crops wilting from leaf rot. Your girl with rashes
    on her little red face…

With a crooked smile, she used her bold voice—
    What say you now, Constable?

He leaned forward as if she were a magnet,
    the corners of his lips curled down, his face tight
    extending his prominent chin. But his eyes lifted.
    Tell me Sister, he said. *You are safe with me.*

Kind sir, there is Isobel, it's mostly her, you already know this—
    I'm not saying her daughter, not Margaret—But Janet and Auntie
    will do whatever she tells them. For today, that's what I know.

You watch your daughter Sir, she may be improving…
    The constable stood back into the shadow again.
    This time he was smiling.

Isobel's Recipe

Turnips, fourteen, waited to be peeled in a colander mouth placed on a cut of wood. Green stalks of celery stacked on each other filled a brown basket. Two sweet onions waited at the table's center. The largest pot from the kitchen, filled with water, sat heating on the outside fire. Isobel loved when the foods were gathered and cut for a fixing. Fresh scents from the kitchen always filled her cottage. That day they weren't in Isobel's cottage.

Other usual ingredients remained off the table, to add later, or to be forgotten. The cooks, without Isobel, sat at Helen Guthrie's square table. Three women and Isobel's daughter, their faces narrow, shoulders curved forward, they sat. Helen, like she did even as a girl, had her favorite knife in her apron pocket.

No bluster or rattle in Helen's kitchen without Isobel.

Helen cut the first onion— slice, slice, chop, chop, slice again. Her rhythm the only sound in the stiff air. No bluster, Isobel gone. Helen's face long, pale, her lips tight. Margaret, still a girl with her own small knife, swiftly slipped thin gray skins from milky white turnips. *You're peeling too fast*, Helen said loudly. Margaret's eyes blinked. Janet striped the strings off celery, trimmed the tips, stood tall, stiff. Auntie did the sweet cabbages, staring down.

It's not what I taught you, Helen snapped.
> *You are not the boss of me*, my mother taught me.
Chop, chop, quick, quick. Slice, slice, slice.
Helen sighed, *Aye, we miss her don't we? King James took her.*
Isobel's at the tollhouse jail, what will become of us?

Note: The Tollhouse in most small towns was also used as a jail.

Isobel's Ghost Speaks

Twenty or thirty of them came for me with ropes and stakes. From hell they hissed—a demon she is. If I could've spoken I would've said the demons were them. To the tollhouse they took me. A cold jail it was. A long time I was there, the rats and me. At the end, there were so many of us from all over Scotland. And it may not be ended.
After the judge condemned me as the devil's wife, they pinned me to the tollhouse wall and strangled me with a metal bit. Strangled me dead. And after it, after, when I saw from the eyes I have now, I saw them take my body and stuff it in a barrel of tar. Aye, they did. Then they burned it. That's how they did it then.

Men carried ropes
and stakes, a barrel of tar
yes, burning would be my fate.

I hadn't seen the girl in months. It was Helen Guthrie told him to blame me, she's the first to accuse me, trying to save her own life and that of her daughter. She was the witch that took us all down. You should know what happened… my story. At first I was calm—I thought no one will believe this. Not after the good I've done here. A lovely baby I delivered, the couple's first born and in a year's time she was dead from fever. Filled with loss and rage, the father said I caused it, the fault was mine, he said, and I thought no one will believe him. They know me, had me to their homes. But all believed it. Aye, they did. All believed it.

That father pointed his finger at me, like Helen told him, accused me, said the devil claimed me, he saw it in a dream-- as sure as the sky was black. The poor mother lost her voice and couldn't look up from the crooked floors. I wasn't a person no more—but a puppet, a demon, the devil's own, that father said, said he would stop me himself. And I've never been so feared, afraid for myself and to see others so feared of me. I prayed to my dear dead husband all through the first nights, listen, I prayed—stuck to my sheets. I prayed to all the heavens, listen, oh listen…

Husband do you hear?
Yes, yes, from the other side
Heaven, it will wait.

The Villagers' Voices 4

After the witches were dead,
people claimed to hear
voices in the gloom
of their dreams.
When there was no fire,
the smell of it woke them.

The witches were dead,
and the town of Forfar settled.
People had suffered enough,
a judge said. Trials ended
and the killings stopped.

Women wove
linen and jute
in their cottages to sell
for country Scotland—

lifting from the burnings
the black plague's scourge
and religious wars
between its own people.

A start to recovery.
After a time, we in Forfar
marked a circle
under an old oak.
Built a stone wall—its perimeter
with a central, standing stone.

Its words, our words, read:

These women were just women,
not witches There be no witches
in County Angus, Forfar, Scotland.

About the Author

Sherri (Sheryll) Bedingfield's poetry has appeared in several anthologies and small press publications including *Caduceus, Journal of Poetry Therapy* and *Connecticut River Review.* She has presented her poetry at Connecticut venues including the Noah Webster House, West Hartford Art League, Word Forge Poetry Series in Hartford, Windsor Art Center, Wintonbury Poetry Series and Yale Book store. One of her poems was selected for the Poetry in the Parks Projects and is displayed at Fernridge Park in West Hartford. She also did the art work that frames the poem. Sherri's work is not just enjoyed locally; she recently read her poetry in Dingle, Ireland. Sherri is the author of *Transitions and Transformations*, published by Antrim House. She did the artwork on its cover. Her poems have been performed by East Haddam Stage Company in *Plays with Poetry*. She acted the roles of two poets from the nineteenth century in a staged performance at the Hill-Stead Museum. Sherri is on the board of the Riverwood Poetry Series. She works as a psychotherapist and a family therapist. She uses art and poetry as creative therapy with some of her clients.